Think Like Jesus

40 Days To Creating A Miracle Mindset

Chad Gonzales

Think Like Jesus: 40 Days To Creating A Miracle Mindset
ISBN 13: 978-0-9853392-3-4
Copyright © 2016, 2021 by Chad Gonzales
All rights reserved.

Preface

When we look at Jesus, there is something innately inside of us that wants to imitate Him because of our union with Him through salvation. When we receive salvation, we become a new creation in Christ Jesus and a new way of living becomes possible. We are spirit beings; as a result, there is a natural longing to experience the supernatural.

As we should, we have looked at Jesus, for He is the prototype of what a man or woman filled with God and empowered by the Holy Spirit can do on the earth. The problem is we have tried to copy His actions without thinking His thoughts and many times the result is a lack of results.

There is a reason the apostle Paul told us in Philippians 2, "Let this mind be in you which was in Christ Jesus." There is a mindset that must be in place in order to make the supernatural natural for us and manifest Heaven while on the earth. Miracles won't become normal in our lives until our thinking lines up with the thoughts of Jesus.

Some would say, "How could we possibly know what Jesus thought?" The answer is simple. What people talk about the most is what they think about the most. Out of the abundance of one's heart they speak!

In reading through the Gospels, especially the book of John, you find that Jesus main topic of conversation was regarding His identity; He talked about it constantly! Through these statements, we find tremendous insight as to why He was able to walk in the supernatural almost effortlessly.

The Bible says in Proverbs 23:7, "As a man thinks in his heart, so is he." Instead of focusing on Jesus actions, we need to focus on His thoughts. If we will simply renew our mind to His thoughts, the actions that produce the miraculous will be a natural by-product.

Day 1: Live From The Supernatural

No one has ascended to heaven but He who came down from heaven, that is the Son of Man who is in heaven. John 3:13

One of the most mind boggling statements Jesus makes is found in John 3:13. Jesus said He was actually living in heaven – while He was standing on the earth!

Even though Jesus was living on the earth, He had learned to live out of Heaven. If you want to operate in the supernatural, you have to live from the supernatural. You have to become more aware of your supernatural resources than your natural resources.

On the earth, there will always be lack – but not in Heaven. Heaven is your home and yet Heaven is where you are to be living from while on the earth. Jesus knew He had access to Heaven's provision and we must as well.

It is why Jesus could look at five loaves of bread and two fish and still see a banquet for ten thousand people. It's the same reason we should look at earthly seed and see abundance or see an inoperable tumor and see a miracle waiting to happen.

We actually live in two worlds. Our spirit is of Heaven and our body is of the earth; therefore, we have access to both. We must view our living situation like Jesus. We must learn through our relationship with the Holy Spirit how to walk on this earth and yet access things from the spirit realm.

It all starts with becoming more aware of the spirit realm than this natural realm. When we become more aware of the spirit realm, we will start to view life's problems in a different way. When our natural eyes see lack, our spiritual eyes will see excess.

Confession: Because of my union with Christ, Heaven is my home and I have no lack.

Scripture reading: Luke 10:9-17

Day 2: God's Gift To The World

If you knew the gift of God and who it is who says to you, "Give Me a drink," you would have asked Him and He would have given you living water. John 4:10

I absolutely love the boldness of Jesus. Jesus knew He was a gift of God and He knew He was a possessor of life. Essentially Jesus said, "If you only knew Who I was, you would have asked for something supernatural."

Because of our union with Christ, we are also a gift to the world. We have been sent by God into the world to set the captives free and manifest God. If you want to do what Jesus did, you must think like Him; you must think this about yourself!

When you stand before someone who needs a touch from God, please know you are a gift from Heaven sent to manifest Heaven in their life. Through Christ, you are the hope for their hopeless situation; you are Christ on the earth.

When you know who you are and what you possess, you can walk in confidence assured of the fact that whatever you face in this world, by God's grace, He has equipped you to handle it. As God sent Jesus into the world, Jesus has sent you into the world. God sent Jesus as a gift and Jesus sent you.

Granted, we are nothing in and of ourselves; we are completely dependent on Jesus. However, we are Christ on the earth; we are His representatives here. If people are going to be set free from the shackles Satan has placed on their lives, it can only from us.

Through your union with Christ, you must see yourself as an answer; you must see yourself as the solution to someone's problem. We must become confident of the Anointed One and His anointing within us so that we can give people a taste of Heaven.

Confession: Through Christ, I am a gift from God to the world. Within me is an answer for life's problems.

Scripture reading: Matthew 9:27-35

Day 3: Food To Finish

My food is to do the will of Him who sent Me, and to finish His work.
John 4:34

After you've gone several hours without food, your body will start screaming at you and regardless of the important tasks you need to take care of, eating will suddenly become your top priority!

In John 4:34, Jesus said His food was doing what God had sent Him to do and finishing it. Not just doing, but also finishing God's will drove Jesus through the obstacles, temptations and pressures of life. Regardless of what came against Jesus, God's plan and purpose for His life was all that mattered. What was the will of God for Jesus? Jesus came to reveal the Father and destroy the works of the devil.

When God's plan for your life becomes number one in your life, you'll find that as you pursue it, God's provision will pursue you. Jesus alluded to this in Matthew 6 when He said, "Don't worry about clothes, food, housing, etc. Seek first the Kingdom of God and all these things will be added to you."

If God's plan for His life was at the forefront of Jesus mind, it should be at the forefront of your mind. When you understand your purpose, it will drive you and provide for you. God didn't send you on a mission and not give you the necessary equipment to get the job done. He gave you His ability, His strength, His self-control, His faith…He gave you Himself.

When the vision is before you, you will stay on track to finish what was started. When you are tempted to drift off course, ask yourself,

"Will this sustain me?" If not, stay away from it because it could keep you from finishing what God sent you to do.

Confession: God's plan for my life sustains and provides for me and I won't let anything get in its way.

Scripture reading: Matthew 6:25-34

Day 4: Six Words For A Miracle

The nobleman said to Him, "Sir, come down before my child dies." Jesus said to him, "Go your way; your son lives." So the man believed the word that Jesus spoke to him, and he went his way. John 4:49-50

Have you ever compared how Jesus responded to situations and how most of us respond? In John 4, we find a man in Capernaum whose son is on his deathbed. He asks Jesus to come pray for his son and Jesus response is "Go your way; your son lives." The nobleman believed Jesus, went home and found his son to be totally healed.

Now let's be honest. If most of us were in Jesus shoes, we would have started a prayer that would have turned into a mini-sermon; however, Jesus said six words. SIX! Why?

Jesus actually believed His words carried weight and authority on the earth. Jesus believed His words spoken in faith carried the same dominion that God's word carried.

Through redemption, Jesus got our speaking back. He gave you a voice of dominion on the earth where you can speak and things of the earth listen and obey.

I have never told my dog to get out of the trash and it took me several minutes of lecturing him to do it. I yell at my dog and say, "Rocky, get out of the trash!" and he not only hears me, but takes off running. It doesn't take much when you know who you are and what is backing you.

See yourself just like Jesus declaring a simple and yet powerful declaration of life over death. People of authority don't need to speak long; they just need to speak strong.

Confession: In Christ, my words carry weight and the things of this earth must obey when I speak in faith.

Scripture reading: Matthew 8:1-4

Day 5: Cooperating With The Holy Spirit

When Jesus saw him lying there, and knew that he already had been in that condition a long time, He said to him, "Do you want to be made well?" John 5:6

In John 5 is the story of the man healed at the pool of Bethesda. In this situation, there were obvious gifts of the Spirit in operation; however, Jesus still had to cooperate.

We don't see Jesus examining the situation and saying, "Okay. This is going to take the word of knowledge, the gift of faith and a working of miracles." No, what you see is absolute confidence in the working of the Holy Spirit in that whatever gift was needed, the Holy Spirit would manifest it.

Jesus wasn't focused on the gifts of the Spirit; He was focused on cooperation with the Spirit. Isn't it interesting that we never see Jesus spend time teaching the disciples about the gifts of the Spirit? In contrast, we see Jesus spend considerable amounts of time teaching the disciples about a relationship with the Holy Spirit.

The gifts of the Spirit are as the Holy Spirit determines; therefore, I'm not focused on a particular gift because I have the Giver of the gifts within me. Why focus on a specific apple when I have the apple tree?

This miracle was certainly initiated by the Holy Spirit because there were many sick people at the pool and He only led Jesus to this particular one. Even though the Holy Spirit prompted Jesus, Jesus had to recognize the leading and then respond in faith. Jesus knew that when He acted, the Holy Spirit would back Him up.

Confession: Whatever the Holy Spirit starts, when I respond to Him, He will finish!

Scripture reading: 2 Kings 4:29-35

Day 6: God Is Still Working

My Father has been working until now and I have been working.
John 5:17

God may have rested from creation, but He's never stopped wanting to work for mankind. God worked with Moses, Abraham, Gideon, Elijah and many others throughout the Bible.

In John 5:17, Jesus said He and the Father were working. Jesus made this statement in the context of gifts of the Spirit in operation at the pool of Bethesda. It should give us tremendous comfort to know God is ALWAYS working for the benefit of His people. However, this reveals to us that if we want results like Jesus, we must work with God like Jesus did.

Friend, the more we put ourselves in a position to fulfill the Great Commission, the more we will see the gifts of the Spirit in operation. The more you begin to be led by the Spirit and step out, the more you will see God step out not only with you, but through you.

In order to step out, you must become aware of your Father's working in you. Philippians 2:13 says, "God works in you to will and do His good pleasure." Colossians 1:29 says, "I strive according to His working that works mightily in me."

We must become more aware of His working than the working of any sickness, lack, shortage or death. We must be more aware of His ability within us than what we see outside of us. God is ready to work, but He needs you to work with Him.

Confession: The Father is always ready to work through me when I am ready to work with Him.

Scripture reading: Acts 14:1-18

Day 7: Relationship Produces Results

The Son can do nothing of Himself, but what He sees the Father do; for whatever He does, the Son also does in like manner. John 5:19

I really like this statement because it shows us why Jesus got results EVERY SINGLE TIME. Jesus didn't look to a book for answers; He looked to the Father for answers.

At the core of Jesus results was a relationship with the Father. The majority of Christians today who desire the supernatural are relying on principles, formulas and step by step guides – but that will never work. If your formula doesn't have God in it, IT WON'T WORK; all you really have are works that don't produce.

Jesus simply copied His Father. It's like any other parent and child relationship; children learn by the example their parents set for them. Jesus wasn't making stuff up; Jesus was copying the Father.
I've seen my son copying me in how to shoot a basketball or throw a football. I've literally seen Jake mimic me down to some of the smallest details while also asking lots of questions. This happens because our relationship provides him the opportunity to get up close and personal and ask the questions of "How?" and "Why?"

Our Father has an open door policy for us. In the same way Jesus had access, you and I have access. We get to determine the extent of our progress in the things of God. Jesus copied the Father so you and I could copy Him. It was Jesus method of operation with all of His disciples including you and me. He showed us what was possible!

Confession: I only do what I see the Father do.

Scripture reading: Acts 3:1-10

Day 8: Make The World Marvel

For the Father loves the Son, and shows Him all things that He himself does; and He will show Him greater works than these, that you may marvel. John 5:20

I love this statement by Jesus for several reasons. Number one, Jesus knew the Father loved Him. When you know God loves you, nothing else matters!

Number two, Jesus was learning from God how to do what only God knew how to do. Through our union with Christ, we have the same access to the Father as Jesus. We can boldly go to God's throne and say, "How does this work?"

Number three, Jesus had an expectation that God was going to show Him even greater miracles. This shows us Jesus didn't know everything.

Jesus wasn't doing life and ministry as God; Jesus was doing life as a man anointed by God. Jesus was looking to the Father not only for answers and provision, but also for greater revelation which would produce greater miracles. If Jesus was expecting more, we should too.

What we know should never be a campground; it should be building blocks for more revelation. Jesus knew there was more available. Jesus knew God wanted to make the world say, "Wow! Did you see that?"

God wants the world to marvel and He wants to make it happen through us, but we must press forward in our fellowship with God. We can't allow anything to get in the way of an increase of revelation knowledge.

Confession: Father, increase my revelation so the world can say with amazement, "Wow!"

Scripture reading: Ephesians 1:15-19

Day 9: A Giver of Life

For as the Father raises the dead and gives life to them, even so the Son gives life to whom He will. John 5:21

Remember that Jesus only did what He saw the Father do. One of the things Jesus saw the Father do was raising the dead...so, that's what Jesus did. Because Jesus was one with God, what flowed through God flowed through Jesus.

You can't give away what you don't possess. Jesus possessed that life and therefore could give it away whenever He wanted.

In the very same manner, you and I have that same life. In John 10:10, Jesus said He came so we could have that life. Jesus came to give us that very life, not only for our benefit, but also for the benefit of others.

Jesus knew He was a carrier and dispenser of the same life that exploded out of God and created the universe; therefore, death was never a match for this life Jesus possessed.

You can never get away from Jesus constant view of relationship with the Father and the miraculous. God was the professor and Jesus was the student. Because of righteousness, Jesus could stand before the Father, watch what was done and with boldness, turn around and replicate it with the very same results.

Don't ever allow death to be viewed greater than the life inside your spirit. It's time we not only see bones grow, but dead bones come to life. It's time for the world to stand in amazement at our great God.

It's time for us to realize that through our union with Christ, we can do what the Father does because we too are His children.

Confession: The same power that flows through Jesus flows through me.

Scripture reading: Matthew 15:29-38

Day 10: Miracles Prove My Mission

The works which the Father has given Me to finish – the very works that I do – bear witness of Me, that the Father has sent Me. John 5:36

Jesus believed miracles were important – extremely important. In Jesus mind, the miracles were proof to the world that God sent Him into the world.

It's interesting to see what we as Christians use as proof that God sent us. We point people to our television programs, book sales, large churches, social media followers and other natural things; Jesus pointed people to the miracles.

When John the Baptist began to question if Jesus was the Christ, Jesus told John about all the people that were healed; Jesus didn't mention anything about the poor people He helped or all the people who were attending His meetings. Jesus proof was never natural; it was always supernatural!

Miracles are the manifestation of God through man and they fill the craving that we innately have as spirit beings. God may speak to us in the still small voice but He speaks through us with miracles!

If you are sent from Heaven, you are sent to manifest Heaven. In the same way a driver's license proves who you are, God's plan was for miracles to be your proof to the world as to whose you are and where you are from. This was the mindset of Jesus and it needs to be our mindset as well.

Miracles get people's attention. Granted, they will not win everyone, but they will cause people to stop and listen. When you determine to be a sent one, God will make sure your identity is proven to the world.

Confession: God sent me to manifest miracles!

Scripture reading: Romans 15:17-19

Day 11: Make Room For
The Impossible

Then Jesus said, "Make the people sit down." Now there was much grass in the place. So the men sat down, in number about five thousand. John 6:10

Much of the modern Church wonders where the miracles have gone; I wonder where the believers have gone.

We owe the world encounters with God and Jesus understood this. In John 6, Jesus set up thousands of people for an encounter with God. Not only was this an opportunity to make the world go "Wow!" it was also a teaching moment for the disciples. Jesus certainly wasn't going to pass this up.

There have been many miracles that we have passed up because when we encountered an impossible situation, we saw lack and backed up; instead of making room for the impossible, we back up and slammed the door shut. When Jesus encountered an impossible situation, He saw provision and went forward.

As part of Jesus preparation, He made the thousands of people sit down – no one was going to miss this miracle. Jesus put Himself in a situation where there was no way out. You'll find with Jesus there never was a plan B – never! Why would you need a secondary option when you know God's Word will work?

Jesus had thousands of people sit down in expectation of a meal in much the same way we would have our dinner guests sit at the table.

With all eyes on Jesus, He turned His eyes to God and acted in faith. Jesus made room for the impossible and God made it overflow.

We must make room for the impossible by getting out of the way. I've had the greatest miracles happen when I put myself in a position where there was no way out but God backing up His Word. It's not fun on your flesh, but the results are amazing. It's the life of faith we have been called to live and it's the life of faith we must live if we are going to manifest the miraculous power of God to a dying world.

Confession: I make room for the impossible when I get my eyes off the situation and onto God.

Scripture reading: 1 Kings 18:20-39

Day 12: Vessels of Life

The words that I speak to you are spirit, and they are life. John 6:63

Jesus knew that His words were spiritual in nature and vessels of life. Our words can produce life or death, blessing or cursing, healing or sickness, prosperity or poverty. Jesus knew He was a possessor of the life of God and one major way He released that life was through His words.

Over the last few decades, there has been much said about the power of our words. Through the abundance of teaching, many have become so focused on the power behind death-filled words that they have forgotten the power behind life-filled words.

In any given situation, Jesus could speak and release the same life of God. It's why Jesus could make a declaration of faith comprised of just a few words and miracles would take place.

If we truly believed in our words like Jesus did, we would make simple, concise commands that actually meant something. I'm convinced the reason many of us are so wordy is that we're trying to convince ourselves something is going to happen.

I'll never forget this particular time I was ministering to a woman in a healing line. I placed my hand on her shoulder and said, "Be healed in Jesus Name." She looked at me and said, "That's all you're going to say?" I said, "What else is needed?" She said, "I just thought you were going to say more." I told her just to check her shoulder and she noticed all the pain was gone. You see, she thought it was a lengthy prayer that would get the job done; however, all that was needed was a command of faith.

Renew your mind to the power of your words - not just the death-filled ones, but also the life-filled ones. Instead of being concerned about not saying the wrong thing, you can speak with boldness the right thing and cause your world to change.

Confession: The words I speak produce life and power!

Scripture reading: Proverbs 12:13-22

Day 13: Fellowship and Revelation

Jesus answered them and said, "My doctrine is not Mine, but His who sent Me." John 7:16

I am a firm believer in education. I love to read books and I love to learn. Most of my spare time is spent reading a book or listening to a podcast because I believe it is important to always be learning. We are blessed in our day and age to have more revelation concerning the Word of God and the ways of God more than any generation before; however, there is always more.

It's important to go to church and make withdrawals from the ministry gifts God has given us. The apostle Paul tells us the ministry gifts are for the equipping and edifying of the believer; however, nothing can take the place of your relationship and fellowship with God.

Both Jesus and the religious leaders of His day had the Old Testament to learn from, but it's obvious Jesus revelation went much deeper than theirs. How? Not because He was Jesus but because He actually spent time fellowshipping with the Father.

You'll never be able to separate the miraculous life of Jesus from His life of fellowship with the Father. Jesus knew God sent Him from Heaven; therefore, it was from God He would always receive instruction and insight. In His life, you see a balance of revelation from the Word and prayer. It's no wonder in reading through the Gospels we find Jesus withdrawing from others and sometimes spending all night in prayer. Many times those all night prayer sessions would lead Jesus into a dire situation and He would perform a tremendous miracle. Why? Because fellowship with God will always produce more revelation and more revelation will always produce more manifestations.

Confession: I will not neglect my fellowship with the Father. He sent me, He instructs me and I receive more revelation every time I am with Him.

Scripture reading: Luke 6:12-19

Day 14: I Am From Him

Then Jesus cried out, as He taught in the temple, saying, "You both know Me, and you know where I am from; and I have not come of Myself, but He who sent Me is true, whom you do not know. But I know Him, for I am from Him, and He sent Me." John 7:28-29

One aspect of Jesus that I absolutely love is His boldness. Jesus was bold because He knew His identity and He knew what He spoke was true.

Jesus said, "I am from Him and He sent Me." Your origin plays a huge role in your identity. Jesus not only originated from Heaven, but He also originated from God because He was born of God.
When you and I were born again, we were literally born from God; we originated from Him and then He sent us into this world. Being conscious of where you are from and your assignment is vital to your success in God. Jesus knew where He was from and what He was sent to do.

A thread that runs throughout the Gospels was Jesus knowing where He was from. In just the Gospel of John, Jesus mentions forty one times that He was sent from Heaven. If you don't know these things, you will wander aimlessly through life not getting any results. You'll fall into the trap, like most Christians, of blaming God for withholding the miraculous.

Remember, we are in this world, but not of it. Things are done differently where we are from. The realities of Heaven are greater than the realities of this world. It's the reason Jesus had a different perspective of life's difficulties than everyone else around Him; as a result, people were able to experience the miraculous through Him.

Confession: I am of God, from God and seeing life through the eyes of God.

Scripture reading: Luke 2:41-52

Day 15: I Am With The Father

And yet if I do judge, My judgement is true; for I am not alone, but I am with the Father who sent Me. John 8:16

Jesus statement in John 8:16 is one that makes your turn your head sideways and go "Huh?" Jesus said, "I am not alone, but I am with the Father who sent Me."

How can you be with someone who sent you somewhere? From a natural perspective it would be like saying, "Lacy sent me to the store and even though I am at the store, I am still with her."

However, from a spiritual perspective, it all makes sense. Remember, we are spirit beings, born from Heaven and yet living on the earth. We are living in two worlds at the same time. Even though I am on the planet earth, in the realm of the spirit, I am still divinely connected to God and with Him.

In the context of this statement, Jesus was talking about God backing Him up. There is a tremendous boldness that rises up within you when you know God is with you – not just in theory, but really knowing God is literally with you.

When you are staring down a tumor or a deformed body part – knowing God is with you will make you say and do some things that you would think were crazy if He wasn't with you.

There have been times I've said something when the anointing was really strong and later I looked back and said, "What was I thinking?" However, that is the reason results happened; I wasn't thinking about the problem because I was completely aware of Him who sent me.

Confession: I am never alone, but I am with the Father who sent Me!

Scripture reading: Ephesians 2:1-10

Day 16: A Superiority Complex

You are from beneath; I am from above.
You are of this world; I am not of this world. John 8:23

In John 8, Jesus basically told the religious leaders that they were from Hell and He was from Heaven. That's pretty blunt, but that is Jesus. Jesus didn't hold back and never took a class in political correctness.

However, there is more to this than Jesus knowing where He was from. Here we see a bit more to it; Jesus knew where He was from was far superior to where they were from.

No matter what storm, disease or financial situation Jesus faced, He knew He was superior. Where He was from was always superior. Who He was with was always superior. Whenever He showed up, everything around Him became inferior.

We must have this mindset. Yes, we walk in love and humility, but we must have a superiority complex when it comes to this world. When we walk into the room, everything changes because of where we are from and Who is with us. If you haven't had a religious person look at you and say, "Who do you think you are?"…then you have some work to do.

There should be an air about you, a confidence surrounding you that you are not of this world and as a result, you are far superior to things originating from this world. You should be looking down at the things of Hell because you are seated at God's right hand in Christ. Regardless of the fact that you are walking on this earth, it doesn't change the truth that you are on assignment from a far superior world.

Confession: I am from above. I am not of this world. I am far superior to anything of this world.

Scripture reading: Matthew 14:22-33

Day 17: Seeing In The Spirit Realm

*I speak what I have seen with My Father and you do
what you have seen with your father. John 8:38*

The spirit realm was extremely real to Jesus; it certainly set Him apart from everyone else. When Jesus was talking to Nicodemus about being born again, Nicodemus was trying to figure out how to get back inside his mother's womb; however, Jesus was talking about being born from Heaven.

When you listen to Jesus speak, He speaks of His relationship with God as if it's just as real as His relationship with the disciples. When Jesus speaks of being sent by God from Heaven, it comes across no different than saying He just left Galilee. How would you feel if you told your friends that you were sent from Heaven? For the vast majority of us, we would probably feel a little silly – but not Jesus.

Because the spirit realm was so real to Jesus, Jesus was able to tap into it and see things in a way other people just couldn't see – not because they weren't able, but because they weren't aware.

If we want to see greater things take place, if we want to see greater works and greater manifestations of God's grace and power, we must open our hearts to the spirit realm. If you are hungry and thirsty for spiritual things, God will fill you up to overflowing; He will let you have as much as you want.

I don't mean just agreeing that it is real, but seriously expanding our thinking and capacity to step further out in the spirit realm. When problems arise, I see through the problem and I see the answer in the realm of which I am not only from, but still live in.

Confession: I do see and I do hear from my Father. The spirit realm is just as real to me as the natural realm.

Scripture reading: 2 Corinthians 4:16-18

Day 18: I Must Reveal God

Jesus answered, "Neither this man nor his parents sinned. But that the works of God should be revealed in him, I must work the works of Him who sent Me while it is day; the night is coming when no one can work." John 9:3-4

Jesus and his disciples had just seen a man blind from birth and the disciples asked why the man was born blind. Jesus said it wasn't anyone's fault. People seem to forget we live in a cursed world where sometimes things happen to people simply because of where we live; however, the focus of Jesus statement was not on the cause, but on the solution.

Essentially, Jesus said, "If this man is going to get healed, I must do something." It certainly wasn't God's will for the man to be blind because God didn't make him blind. It's always and I mean always God's will for people to be healed, but in order for God's will to be manifest, it will take a man or woman willing to work the works of God.

It may seem arrogant, but it's not. Jesus knew what His purpose was; He was a man on a mission from Heaven to manifest Heaven and destroy the works of the devil in people's lives. The people from this earth can't do anything about it, but people from Heaven can. We are superior to this world including the demons and the problems in it.

If Heaven is going to be manifest on the earth, we must do it. It won't happen just because God wants it; God gave the earth to man and it's our responsibility to take the mandate from God, backed with the power of God, to set people free from the bondages of Satan. God needs us to manifest Him!

Confession: For the world to see the works of God, I must allow God to work through me.

Scripture reading: Luke 4:16-19

Day 19: Releasing The Anointing

When He had said these things, He spat on the ground and made clay with the saliva; and He anointed the eyes of the blind man with the clay. And He said to him, "Go, wash in the pool of Siloam" (which is translated, Sent). So he went and washed, and came back seeing.
John 9:6-7

Jesus was a master at releasing the anointing with skill and releasing it on purpose. If we want to get the same results as Jesus, we must become skilled as well.

In John 9, Jesus met the man born blind. In the beginning of their encounter, the blind man isn't in faith, so Jesus helped move the man into a position to release his faith and lock in on the anointing. Remember, Jesus only did what He saw the Father do.

There have been times when I was ministering to someone and just like a flash, in my mind, I see myself doing something; when I step out in faith on what I saw, it always works. It's the Holy Spirit enlightening me and giving me instruction. In this situation with the blind man, Jesus made mud, anointed the man's eyes and then gave him something simple to do: go wash in the pool of Siloam.

Think about the command Jesus gave. Jesus told a blind man to go somewhere. Many people would say that was cruel, but it was actually love; Jesus was getting this man to his miracle. This required many steps of faith by the blind man to do what Jesus asked; however, in his obedience, the man unknowingly was releasing his faith and accessing the power.

When Jesus gave the command, the anointing was within it. Jesus knew He was anointed with the Holy Spirit and anointed with power to heal all those who were oppressed by the devil. Jesus knew He could release the anointing through the laying on of hands and through words. In this situation, Jesus released the anointing with words and with the man's obedience, his action tapped into the anointing and he was completely healed.

We must get to the point where we are so in tune with the voice of the Holy Spirit, we say what God wants us to say and do what God wants us to do so we can connect people to the anointing – on purpose!

Confession: The words God tells me to speak carry the anointing. When I speak His Word, I'm releasing the anointing which will destroy anything of the devil.

Scripture reading: Mark 8:22-25

Day 20: I Am Light

As long as I am in the world, I am the light of the world. John 9:5

Light can illuminate, it can create and it can destroy. As the light of the world, Jesus did all three. Remember, Jesus knew He wasn't from the earth. He knew He was superior because of His union with God, His origin from God and His superior birthplace.

Wherever Jesus went, He brought revelation to closed minds. He created new eyes and ears, new limbs and organs and fixed anything else that was missing or broken because of the glory of God that filled Him to the full.

Now, because of our union with Christ, we are the light of the world. We are the light in the dark places. We are Christ on the earth! Where we go, darkness flees because darkness can never overtake light – NEVER!

This is why cancer and other diseases should scream in fear when we walk in the room. The light of God that emanated from Jesus when he was transfigured on the mountain is the same light that's within our spirit waiting to be released on darkness.

I am convinced that if we saw in the spirit realm, you would see Christians as massive lights and the more revelation a Christian walks in, the brighter that light is.

We should not only be a beacon of light that represents hope in the world, we should also be a laser that creates life and absolutely obliterates the strongholds of darkness. The same glory that was within Jesus is in you now because of redemption. It's time for your light to shine bright!

Confession: Christ lives in me! I am a light in this world bringing revelation to people's minds and healing to their bodies. The darkness is scared of me!

Scripture reading: John 1:1-4

Day 21: I Know His Voice

And when he brings out his own sheep, he goes before them; and the sheep follow him, for they know his voice. John 10:4

I think it's safe to say Jesus knew the voice of God; although, it wasn't because He was Jesus. Jesus knew the voice of God because Jesus spent time with God and continued expanding and opening His heart to God.

It's not hard to know the voice of God; actually, as a born again child of God, you do know His voice. He is your Father and you are His child. Jesus made it very plain and clear: the sheep know the voice of the Shepherd.

As the apostle John said, "You are of God little children." You were born of God and because He is your Father, your spirit man knows His voice; the problem is your soul (mind, will and emotions) does not. This is why so much time is spent telling us in the New Testament about the importance of renewing our mind to the realities of Heaven.

We have to purpose not to be conformed to this world in our thinking that hearing from God is hard and abnormal. Jesus showed us that a relationship with God was very normal, natural and more real than the relationships He had with His disciples.

The more you open your mind to the truth that you do know God's voice, the more your mind will begin to align with your spirit and you will start picking up what God is saying.

God is a spirit and we are a spirit; therefore, it should be normal for us to hear from Him.

Confession: I do know the voice of God because He is my Father. He is always speaking and I am always hearing. It is normal for me to hear from Him.

Scripture reading: Colossians 3:1-3

Day 22: Faith In The Command

Therefore My Father loves Me because I lay down My life that I may take it again. No one takes it from Me, but I lay it down of Myself. I have power to lay it down and I have power to take it again. This command I have received from My Father. John 10:17-18

Jesus had so much trust in the Father that He was unrelenting in His mission to fulfill it – no matter what the natural circumstances looked like. God had given Jesus the command of giving His life for the world; however, God never gives a command without also giving the power to fulfill the command. He gave Jesus the power to not only lay down His life but also the power to raise Himself up. Think about this.

For three years, Jesus not only had the cross to face, but also separation from God – which would result in spiritual torture in Hell. Despite all of that, Jesus was unwavering in fulfilling the mission all based on a command from God.

How many times have we faced a situation and questioned the result even though God had given us the power and command to overcome it? How many times have we faced sickness or lack, armed with the authority of Heaven and yet begin to doubt.

We must be as confident in God's Word as Jesus. Jesus viewed a word from God for what it was: a carrier of power to go forth and fulfill what it was sent to do regardless of what enemy tried to stop it. God's Word is unstoppable and unchangeable!

Miracles aren't always pretty until they happen. We must become unflinching in the face of negative situations when we are armed with a Word from God.

Jesus was willing to die an excruciating death based on a promise that He could take His life back again after three days. Would you be willing to die based on a promise?

This is the type of faith in God it takes to accomplish the miracles Jesus experienced on the earth – and that faith won't come through steps and formulas – that faith will come from fellowship with the Father. This faith was grounded in love and a byproduct of their fellowship. Jesus knew God loved Him so much that Jesus literally trusted Him with His life and if He could trust God with His life, Jesus could trust Him in any other situation.

Confession: I'll stick with the Word regardless of what the situation looks like because God's Word always comes to pass when I act on it in faith.

Scripture reading: Philippians 2:5-13

Day 23: Fear Does Not Deserve A Reaction

Therefore the sisters sent to Him saying, "Lord, behold, he whom You love is sick." When Jesus heard that, He said, "This sickness is not unto death, but for the glory of God, that the Son of God may be glorified through it." Now Jesus loved Martha and her sister and Lazarus. So when He heard that he was sick, He stayed two more days in the place where He was. John 11:3-6

When Jesus heard of Lazarus being sick, He didn't react in fear; it's important to note because He loved this family. Typically, if there was an accident that happened with one of our family members, as soon as we heard the information, we would drop what we were doing, allow our emotions to take over and react in fear.

WE ARE NEVER TO REACT IN FEAR; WE ARE TO RESPOND TO THE FATHER! We respond in faith to God's report and His report says we always have the victory in Christ!

It's interesting that after Jesus found out Lazarus was very sick, Jesus decided to stay where He was at for two more days. Jesus knew the seriousness of the situation because the Holy Spirit revealed to Him that Lazarus was dead. Even after knowing Lazarus was dead, Jesus remained calm and immovable. When you already know you have the victory, there is no need to be moved by circumstances.

You can see very quickly if you are spirit-led or flesh-led by how you immediately respond to bad news. When you hear bad news, you need to take a deep breath, grab hold of your thoughts and emotions and refrain from reacting. Put your mind on the realities of God and look to the Holy Spirit as to what to do. If you are in the process of eating, finish your meal. If you are washing your car, finish washing your car.

Whatever you are in the process of doing, finish it. Don't let the devil see you reacting to the situation he has caused. You go when you're ready – not when the situation tells you to go because nothing in this world should be ruling us.

Confession: I do not react to fear, but I respond to the Father. In every situation, I always have the victory in Christ.

Scripture reading: Mark 5:35-43

Day 24: A Stench Can't Stop My Declaration

Jesus said, "Take away the stone." Martha, the sister of him who was dead, said to Him, "Lord, by this time there is a stench, for he has been dead four days." Jesus said to her, "Did I not say to you that if you would believe you would see the glory of God?"
John 11:39-40

When Jesus heard Lazarus was sick, he stayed where he was at two more days; Jesus wasn't moved by the circumstances. His response was to declare the word of God and then wait until the Holy Spirit told Him to leave.

Later, Jesus told the disciples He was going to raise Lazarus from the dead. On Jesus way to the tomb, He was stopped by Martha and in response to Martha's emotions, Jesus declared, "Your brother Lazarus will rise again."

When Jesus finally got to the tomb, He told the people to remove the stone. Martha's response was, "It's been four days and now there is a stench!" It's like she thought raising someone from the dead was easier after one day than four days!

Yet even after Martha's statement of unbelief, it didn't deter Jesus because two days before, He had already declared the outcome. Jesus had opportunities to change His confession but He kept saying the same thing; even a four day old stench didn't move Him! It may have moved his nose, but it didn't move His stance on His declaration of faith. When Jesus confessed Lazarus would rise, it became His possession and would remain His unless He let it go.

Miracles aren't pretty until they happen – and in this case didn't smell pretty either! We must be like Jesus in that when we declare God's Word, we believe God's Word and we don't allow anything to move us from our declaration. Remember, we are Christ on the earth. We are God's mouthpiece on this planet. We are the prophet of our lives and we will have what we say.

Confession: In the face of impossible situations, I do not change my confession of my possession. I will have what I say!

Scripture reading: Mark 11:10-22-26

Day 25: Just As My Father Told Me

For I have not spoken on My own authority; but the Father who sent Me gave Me a command, what I should say and what I should speak. And I know that His command is everlasting life. Therefore, whatever I speak, just as the Father has told me, so I speak. John 12:49-50

Jesus valued God's Word. If God spoke it, Jesus did not err from it. Never forget that Jesus obedience always stemmed from His knowing God's absolute, unwavering love for Him. Every command given to Jesus was out of love for Him and as a result, Jesus had an unwavering trust for the Father.

If we want to see the miraculous, we have to see the spoken word of God just like Jesus did. God's Word is life. Jesus did not add to it nor take away from it; just as God told Him, that is what Jesus said.

It's interesting to note that when Jesus faced the death of a loved one, it didn't change what He spoke. When He was opposed by the political and religious leaders, Jesus didn't suddenly become politically correct. When Jesus knew people were offended because of what He said, He didn't run after them and change His teaching. In Jesus mind, what God said is what He said and nothing would ever change it.

You can see why Jesus always moved in the miraculous and the supernatural was natural for Him. People, circumstances and emotions never changed what He said.

When God speaks, His word goes forth unhindered and produces results. If we will renew our mind as Jesus to the integrity and power of God's Word, we would see the same results.

Confession: I only say what the Father has told me to say and as a result, I will see the victory – every single time!

Scripture reading: Isaiah 55:10-11

Day 26: Love That Produces

A new commandment I give to you, that you love one another; as I have loved you, that you also love one another. By this all will know that you are My disciples, if you have love for one another."
John 13:34-35

Love will cause you to do some crazy things because love enables you to see some things you wouldn't see otherwise. In John 13, Jesus gives the command to love others as He loved us. Remember that Jesus told us that if we had seen Him, we had seen the Father. The love Jesus was showing toward us is the love God was showing toward Him.

Because we love people the way Jesus loves us, it means we will have to respond differently in situations that require the anointing. If a catastrophe strikes a loved one, the natural response is to become emotional and get in fear – but that is a selfish response. It is a response that is not for them, but for us because we don't want to lose that individual.

The response of love in a dire situation is always a response of faith; you cannot separate the two. If you truly love a person, you'll rule over your emotions and thoughts so you can release the anointing in that situation and bring victory for that person.

Love others as Jesus loves us. How would Jesus respond if we were in trouble? We can see a great example of it when Jesus and the disciples were in the boat during a great storm. Love stayed calm. Love stayed in control and therefore took control over the storm.

Be a master of love not only for yourself, but also for others and you will be in position to master your situation with a love that will always produce a miracle.

Confession: Because I love like God loves, I will produce the correct response that will release the anointing.

Scripture reading: 1 John 3:14-22

Day 27: I Look Like My Father

If you had known Me, you would have known My Father also; and from now on you know Him and have seen Him. John 14:7

Jesus was radical in His statements because He was radical in His thinking. Can you imagine telling people when they see you, they see God? Well, if you want results like Jesus, then you should. Jesus in spirit was like God in every way. Jesus knew Genesis 1:26-27 which states man was made in the image and likeness of God.

When you are born of God, you are just like your Daddy. You take on His very life and nature; you get His DNA. This is what we read about in Galatians 5 regarding the traits of God. We have His love, joy, peace, patience, kindness, goodness, faith, gentleness and self-control. God made us to be like Him.

Jesus knew these things. These truths were such a reality to Jesus that it affected His view of Himself. Philippians 2 tells us that Jesus did not think it robbery to be made equal with God. Never forget that although Jesus was God, He was doing life completely as a man.

Because of our union with Christ, we can say the same thing. Outwardly, we are different; yet inwardly, the real us is just like Jesus. 1 John 4:17 says, "As He is, so are we in this world."

We are God's representatives on this earth. If the world is going to experience Him, we must manifest Him, but we won't fully do it without seeing ourselves in His image and likeness.

Confession: Because of my union with Christ, if you've seen me,

you've seen the Father. Because I only say what the Father says, if you hear me, you've heard Him.

Scripture reading: Colossians 1:12-20

Day 28: The Father In Me Does The Works

Do you not believe that I am in the Father, and the Father in Me?
The words that I speak to you I do not speak on My own authority;
but the Father who dwells in Me does the works. John 14:10

Jesus was what I would call "God-inside minded." Jesus didn't just believe God was on the throne in Heaven; Jesus also fervently believed God was living within Him.

The majority of Christians believe the reason Jesus produced the miraculous was simply because He was Jesus – but that is not true. There is no Scripture to back up that belief; however, Jesus explicitly tells us how the miracles were happening in John 14:10. Jesus said, "The Father who dwells in Me does the works."

This statement blows holes in most people's theology and yet it's the reason most Christians aren't seeing the supernatural the way they should. We need to be conscious of God in us. It can't be just a theory; it must be a reality!

Because God is in me, His power is in me, His ability is in me and everywhere I go, He is there to work through me. The apostle Paul said in Colossians 1:29, "I labor according to His working which works in me mightily."

We must become God-inside minded. Instead of viewing God as a million miles away, view Him as right under your nose; see Him within you. The apostle Paul told the Corinthians repeatedly that they were the temple of God. It is a vital truth! It was God's desire to get into man; it was the purpose of redemption. Under the Old Covenant, God resided in a wood box; under the New Covenant, God resides in men recreated in Him.

The more aware we are of God within us, the greater we will see God moving through us.

Confession: God is working in me and through me!

Scripture reading: 2 Corinthians 6:16-18

Day 29: Miracles Are The Proof

Believe Me that I am in the Father and the Father in Me, or else believe Me for the sake of the works themselves.   John 14:11

What you think about the most is what you talk about the most and we can readily see that with Jesus. We know His identification with God was vitally important because Jesus always talked about it.

Jesus identification with the Father was so important in fulfilling God's master plan that God gave Jesus proof of this union: miracles. Jesus said, "If you don't believe the teaching, believe the manifestations!" God will never give you a message without proof to back it up.

The message we have been given doesn't make sense in this world; therefore, it needs something that appeals to people's natural senses to help convince them of the validity of the message.

This is why we need miracles. The Church must have miracles because the world is crying out for something real. The world is desperate for real manifestations from the sons of God.

God never meant for us to deliver a supernatural message without supernatural proof. The more we begin to see our union with God, the more we will see miracles on demand because God wants to reveal Himself to the world.

From the very beginning of time, it has been God's heart cry to become one with mankind; it was the sole purpose of redemption. The world needs to see what the heart of God has already provided.

We see this in the Great Commission - that was the purpose of the signs, wonders and miracles! The signs were to authenticate the message and the messenger so the hearer knew the Gospel message was true.

Confession: The miracles God works through me proves His union with me.

Scripture reading: Mark 16:15-20

Day 30: The Same Works

Most assuredly, I say to you, he who believes in Me, the works that I do he will do also; and greater works than these he will do, because I go to My Father. John 14:12

The reason Jesus was able to do the miracles He did was because of His union with God. Jesus would make statements such as, "It's the Father within Me who does the works" and "If you don't believe that I am in the Father, believe the works."

Jesus union with God was such a reality that it shaped His thinking which shaped His actions.

Jesus further knew what His purpose was on the earth: to redeem mankind. The desire of God was for Jesus to restore us back to God's original plan for man in that God would be one with them again.

Jesus knew that because of His union with the Father, the miraculous was possible; therefore, because of redemption, it would make us one with Him, thus paving the way for the miraculous in our life as well.

If Jesus was confident in this, we should be as well. Jesus believed that union with God produced miracles from God not only in His life, but ultimately in our lives as well.

When you are faced with a situation needing a miracle, the first thing that should come to mind is your union with Christ. Miracles are normal for the person united to God in Christ!
Jesus said we could do the very same works. Either Jesus was lying or telling the truth; I believe He was telling the truth. If I have the

same union with God as Jesus does, then I am qualified to do the same works. When it becomes a reality in our mind, it will become a reality in our daily walk on the earth.

Confession: Because I am one with Christ, the same miracles He did, I can do also. Miracles are normal for me because of my union with Him.

Scripture reading: John 14:10-14

Day 31: The Ultimate Teacher

But the Helper, the Holy Spirit, whom the Father will send in My name, He will teach you all things, and bring to your remembrance all things that I said to you. John 14:26

Jesus was our example of how to do life on the earth. Jesus was doing life as a man. He had to renew His mind like us and keep his soul and body under subjection like us. He didn't show up on the earth knowing everything. The Bible tells us in Luke 2 that Jesus grew in stature and in wisdom. God doesn't grow in wisdom, but a man does.

In John 14:26, Jesus begins to introduce the disciples and us to our greatest ally in this world: the Holy Spirit. Jesus said the Holy Spirit would teach us all things.

As far as writings, all Jesus had was the Old Testament but He had the Holy Spirit to teach Him and give Him revelation from the Word. I thank God for anointed preachers and teachers through which the Holy Spirit can teach us and equip us, but we must also learn to hear from Him in our daily walk with God.

There will be times when it's just you and the Holy Spirit; you won't have anyone to stand there and hold your hand or declare faith words for you. There will be situations that you have never encountered before and no one else is there to help you. It is in these situations we must be positioned to be taught by Him, but that means in our day to day walk, we must stay aware of Him.

Jesus depended on the Holy Spirit to teach Him what to do and what to say; it is the reason Jesus with pinpoint accuracy got results every single time a miracle was needed.

Some situations we read about in the Gospels were similar and yet Jesus response was sometimes different because the Holy Spirit knew what was needed for that exact situation. We must not assume because the situation is similar that the response should be the same. Sometimes Jesus spoke, sometimes He laid hands and sometimes He gave a command.

The Holy Spirit is a genius and He will make you look like a genius in the supernatural too if we will simply look to Him in every situation. Remember we are to say what He says and do what He does – and nothing else.

Confession: The Holy Spirit is my teacher and He will teach me all that I need to know. He will guide me into the miraculous!

Scripture reading: 1 Corinthians 2:9-16

Day 32: A Permanent Address

As the Father loved Me, I also have loved you; abide in My love. If
you keep My commandments, you will abide in My love, just as I
have kept My Father's commandments and abide in His love.
John 15:9-10

If your life isn't rooted and grounded in the love God has for you, you will not accomplish much for Him. In Jesus case, it was the direct opposite; nothing could move Him nor separate Him from the love God had for Him.

Jesus said "As the Father loved Me, I also have loved you; abide in My love." Jesus was always showing us what was possible on the earth as a man united to God and anointed by God. In addition, Jesus never asked us to do anything He didn't do.

Jesus went on to say, "Abide in my love as I abide in His love." Perfect love casts out all fear. There is a reason Jesus could look Hell straight in the eye and not be moved because He was abiding in the love of the Father.

The word abide refers to "dwelling in a place without leaving; to take up a permanent residence." In other words, once you move in, you never move out; it is your permanent address.

This goes further than just loving people and not getting offended. I'm talking about being so rooted in His love that when Satan comes against you, you don't even bat an eye. Abiding in His love is abiding in His victory. Abiding in His love is abiding in the realm of where nothing is impossible. God's commands produce victory and life for us and are always from the standpoint of love for us.

When we obey what God tells us to do, we aren't allowing ourselves to be moved by the impossible; we remain in a place of faith which causes us to remain in a place where all things are possible. When we hold fast to God's Word, we stay grounded in His love for us and remain where the supernatural is natural.

Confession: I will stay rooted and grounded in God's love for me. It is the place I choose to dwell. In the face of adversity, I will not change addresses! I will not be moved!

Scripture reading: Ephesians 3:14-21

Day 33: The Power Will Expose Sin

If I had not done among them the works which no one else did, they would have no sin; but now they have seen and also hated both Me and My Father. John 15:24

The works Jesus refers to are the miracles of which He did. Jesus wasn't talking about taking care of the poor; Jesus was talking about the power of God being manifested.

Notice Jesus said "If I had not done among them the works which no one else did, they would have no sin." The power of God on display will expose sin and people's need of a Savior. It is what light does. When the lights are turned on, it exposes what has been under darkness.

Jesus understood that not only were the miracles necessary to set people free as well as prove His union with God, the miracles were also necessary to expose darkness.

If there ever was a time in which sin needed to be exposed, it is today – in the world and in the Church.

If there ever was a time in which the Church needed a great awakening, it is today! The modern Church needs a big slap in the face to wake up to who we are in Christ, repent of the laxness and unrighteousness we have allowed in our churches and manifest the miraculous power of God.

Jesus understood this and we must too. He was adamant about manifesting the power of God because He knew the world needed it and the religious people needed it. Why? When the power is manifest, it gives people an opportunity to see the Father.

It doesn't mean everyone will believe because not everyone will. If they all didn't believe Jesus, they won't all believe us; however, everyone must be given the opportunity to make a choice and that means we have to flip the switch and manifest Heaven on the Earth.

Confession: The world and the Church need to see the miraculous and because of my union with God, they will see it through me. I will do my part in awakening the Church and opening the eyes and hearts of the world!

Scripture reading: John 10:30-39

Day 34: The Realities of God

However, when He, the Spirit of truth, has come, He will guide you into all truth; for He will not speak on His own authority, but whatever He hears He will speak; and He will tell you things to come.
John 16:13

There will never be such a thing as a life of miracles without a life led by the Holy Spirit; it's just not possible. It's a life led by the Holy Spirit that will lead you into miracles because He will help you to think like God.

Jesus said, "The Holy Spirit will guide you into all truth." The word truth is the Greek word aletheia which means reality. Truth is something that cannot be changed or altered. One of the main jobs of the Holy Spirit is to guide us into the realities of Heaven - how Heaven operates and how Heaven sees things. We must never forget we are not of this world. Heaven is our home and our citizenship.

Jesus was doing life on the earth as a man. Even though He was seeing natural circumstances, He was able to rely on the Holy Spirit to help Him see things through the perspective of Heaven. The things of this world are always subject to change.

The apostle Paul said we are not to look to things that are seen but the things that are unseen because the things that are seen are temporary, but the things that are not seen are eternal.

We will have trials and persecutions in this life and as a result, we will have opportunities presented to walk in life's facts or walk in Heaven's truths. If we will look to the Holy Spirit as Jesus did, He will guide us into what is true so we can act accordingly. When we walk according to Heaven's realities, we release the working of the Holy Spirit into our world.

Confession: The Holy Spirit guides me into Heaven's realities. As I see through the lens of Heaven, I what is possible on the Earth.

Scripture reading: 2 Corinthians 4:16-18

Day 35: The Father Is Always With Me

Indeed the hour is coming, yes, has now come, that you will be scattered, each to his own, and will leave Me alone. And yet I am not alone, because the Father is with Me. These things I have spoken to you, that in Me you may have peace. In the world you will have tribulation; but be of good cheer, I have overcome the world.
John 16:32-33

If we want to walk in the supernatural, we must know we are never alone. People are fickle; they will come and they will go. Usually the ones that tell you they are with you until Jesus comes are usually the ones that are with you until they get offended at you.

Jesus told the disciples there was a time coming when they would all leave Him, but even though they would be gone, He wouldn't be alone – God would still be with Him.

To walk in the supernatural and live a life of miracles, there will be many times you will find yourself seemingly all alone. I've had ministers I used to look up to tell me I needed to be careful in how I was believing God. Some would tell me I was going too far and I needed to use wisdom, but it was simply because they weren't willing to step out beyond what they knew so they could experience more of God.

In those times, you must know God is with you. When things around you look a little scary, you must know God is with you. When you are facing the impossible, you must know God is with you. God with you and in you must be a constant reality in your life. How could you ever be afraid when you know God is with you?

Jesus revealed that this was the reason that in every situation, He was full of peace, always had joy and always overcame. Jesus was modeling for us His relationship with God and the relationship that was available for us.

When you know God is with you, you can face tribulation with a smile on your face, joy in your heart, and peace in your mind because you know you have already won.

Confession: God is always with me; He has never left me. As a result, I am full of peace and full of joy because I know that what I am facing is already defeated. In Christ, I always have the victory.

Scripture reading: Hebrews 13:5-6

Day 36: Not Of This World

I have given them Your word and the world has hated them because they are not of the world, just as I am not of the world. John 17:14

One of the major components of Jesus identity and a major topic of Jesus conversations was that He was not from this earth. In John 17, Jesus is praying in the Garden of Gethsemane and says that just as He is not of this world, we are not of this world.

Just like Jesus, we must know our origin is of Heaven; we must know we are aliens in this world. Because we are born of God, we must be on guard of our identity.

Everything in this world will try to persuade you that you are merely human – but don't take the bait. As a new creation in Christ Jesus, you are born of God.

Not only will the world try to persuade you away from your true identity, it will also try to persuade you away from your dominion. Because we are from Heaven, we have dominion over this world; we are free of every system in the world. The healthcare system, the financial system, the political system…all the systems of this world can't determine what you and I can possess or pursue for God.

When God created Adam and Eve, He made them in His likeness and image and then gave them dominion over the world. Just because Adam messed up, it didn't change God's plan; Jesus came to restore not only our identity, but also our dominion and authority.
Where we are from allows us to live above the impossible. The barriers this world faces are simply stepping stones for us. When

the economy falls apart, it doesn't cause us to fall apart because we operate according to Heaven's economy. When disease begins to ravage through people, it doesn't affect us because we are immune to it. We stare at death and command it to go. We look down at lack and declare abundance.

We are not of this world. We are superior to everything in this world because we are born of God and born out of Heaven; we were sent to this earth to do a job and then head back home.

Confession: I am not of this world and I have dominion over the systems of this world. This world does not own me nor does it rule me; because I am born of God, I rule it.

Scripture reading: 1 John 4:1-6

Day 37: Perfect In One

And the glory which You gave Me I have given them, that they may be one just as We are one: I in them, and You in Me; that they made be made perfect in one, and that the world may know that You have sent Me, and have loved them as You have loved Me. John 17:22-23

John 17 is one of my favorite chapters in the Bible because we gain tremendous insight into the mind of Christ. While Jesus is praying in the Garden of Gethsemane, He basically spills the beans as to all the things that are important to His success and our success in the supernatural. Not only does Jesus repeatedly state He is not of this world, He also repeatedly states His union with God.

Jesus prayed that you and I would be one with Him and the Father. Think about it. This is what Jesus went to the cross for! We know it became a reality because the apostle Paul said in Colossians 2:9-10, "Jesus is the fullness of the Godhead bodily and you are complete in Him."

Jesus said because of that union, you and I would be made perfect; after all, if you are one with Him, you'd have to be perfect and complete because God is perfect. This is where righteousness stems from.

Jesus never questioned His standing with the Father because Jesus was unified with Him. Because you are the righteousness of God in Christ, you are complete – nothing missing! We are the righteousness of God in Christ. We are complete in Him! The only thing we must do is grow in revelation of who we are in Christ so we can mature in these realities.   We must renew our mind so we're no longer conformed to this world, but conformed to the realities of Heaven.

Confession: Because of redemption, I am one with God. Through my union with my Father, I have been made righteous, perfect and complete.

Scripture reading: Colossians 2:6-10

Day 38: I Know Who I Am

Jesus therefore, knowing all things that would come upon Him, went forward and said to them, "Whom are you seeking?" They answered Him, "Jesus of Nazareth." Jesus said to them, "I am He." And Judas, who betrayed Him, also stood with them. Now when He said to them, "I am He," they drew back and fell to the ground. John 18:4-6

If we want to operate as Jesus did, we must know our identity as Jesus did. Without question, Jesus knew who He was, where He was from, what He possessed and with Whom He was united.

When the officers questioned Jesus identity in the Garden, Jesus simple response of "I am" sent them tumbling backwards. This wasn't just a response from the head; this was a response from His heart.

When you fully know who you are and declare it, it is a powerful force from your mouth that will knock the demonic forces assembled against you on their back. Why? Because you are someone united with God! When you declare who you are, you are declaring who God is!

If you've seen me, you've seen the Father. God made man in His image and likeness. After God formed his body, He put Himself into man and the angels began to wonder "Who is this man that you are mindful of him?" I'm sure there was a moment when all of Heaven was silent as they watched this miracle unfold.

I can see the angels looking at God and looking at man and thinking "Which one is which?" because God made man identically like Him so man could represent Him on the earth. Man was made to operate on God's level while dependent on God. We see this in Jesus with absolute perfection.

We must know who we are. We must stop watering it down for the sake of religious correctness. If we want to do what Jesus did, we must think like He thought.

Confession: To declare who I am is to release God on the scene. I am one with God!

Scripture reading: Psalm 8:4-6

Day 39: For This Reason I Was Born

Pilate therefore said to Him, "Are You a king then?" Jesus answered, "You say rightly that I am a king. For this cause I was born, and for this cause I have come into the world, that I should bear witness to the truth. Everyone who is of the truth hears My voice." John 18:37

As Jesus is standing before Pilate, He has an opportunity to save Himself from being crucified on the cross. When Pilate asked Jesus if He was a king, Jesus could have passed on the question, but He didn't. Jesus knew who He was and where He was from. Jesus knew His identity and He knew His purpose for being sent from Heaven to the Earth. Jesus response is wonderful. He says, "You say rightly I am a king and for this cause I was born…"

Jesus knew why He was born; Jesus knew His purpose was to come into the world and bear witness of God's realities. It was knowing His purpose that Jesus could stand before death and not be moved; in Jesus case, He had to move toward it.

Jesus knew why He was born; do you know why you were born? It's a common question I hear from people. "Why was I born?" "What is my purpose here on the Earth?" I don't know your specific purpose but I can tell you it's foundation is exactly what Jesus said His purpose was: to bear witness to the truth.

God redeemed us through Jesus death, burial and resurrection. He birthed us from Heaven and sent us into the world to continue to be a witness for Jesus. For this reason, you and I were born!

You will never be able to be a witness for Jesus in word only. The apostle Paul said in Romans 15 that it was through mighty signs and wonders he fully preached the Gospel of Jesus. Jesus repeatedly said that the miracles He did were the witness to the reality that God sent Him.

When we know why we are born then we know what we need to do. You were born for such a time as this! You were born to bear witness to the resurrection of Jesus Christ! You were born for the miraculous!

Confession: For this reason I was born so that I could bear witness to the truth of Jesus Christ!

Scripture reading: Luke 7:11-22

Day 40: No Power Against Me

Then Pilate said to Him, "Are You not speaking to me? Do You not know that I have power to crucify You, and power to release You?" Jesus answered, "You could have no power at all against Me unless it had been given you from above. Therefore the one who delivered Me to you has the greater sin." John 19:10-11

Jesus stands before Pilate with one last opportunity to save Himself. By this point, Jesus has been severely beaten, whipped and had a crown of massive thorns pushed down upon and through His scalp. With a body covered in bruises, blood and exposed flesh, Jesus still stands before Pilate with an attitude of dominion.

Pilate says to Jesus, "Do you not know that I have the power to crucify you or set you free?" Jesus response is breathtaking. Jesus says, "You have no power against Me."

Remember in John 10, Jesus said, "No one takes My life from Me. I have power to lay it down and power to take it again." No one from this Earth had anything over Jesus. No man could kill Jesus unless Jesus gave them the power to do so.

No sickness, no disease and no human being could take Jesus out unless He gave permission. If this is the case for Jesus, this is also the case for you and I.

We have been made in the image of God and sent from Heaven to the Earth. God lives within us and works through us! All authority in Heaven and Earth has been given to us. We have been given the Name of Jesus, the Name that is above all, at which everything must bow. We have been seated with Christ at the very right hand of God, far above all principality, power, might and dominion. We have been made alive together with Christ, complete in Him, united with the Father and anointed by the Holy Spirit. NOTHING SHALL BY ANY MEANS HARM US WITHOUT OUR PERMISSION!

We should stand as Jesus did before every demonic force on the earth and stare down at them with absolute complete dominion as their master and our slave.

We have been made to reign as kings in this life! It is time to represent our King!

Confession: Nothing in this world has power over me because I am not of this world!

Scripture reading: Romans 6:1-14

About The Author

Chad is on a mission to help the Church elevate it's standard to that of Jesus Himself. It is his heart for the Church to awaken to who they are and manifest Heaven on the Earth as true children of God.

With a strong emphasis on one's identity in Christ and healing, Chad declares the Word of God with great boldness and without compromise. As a result, miraculous healings are common in his ministry including blind eyes, deaf ears, tumors dissolved, chronic diseases healed, short bones growing out and much more.

For more information about this ministry and to view available media and books, please visit:

www.ChadGonzales.com
www.Facebook.com/ChadGonzalesMinistries
Youtube.com/ChadGonzalesMinistries

The Healing Academy is an outreach of Chad Gonzales Ministries to help the everyday believer learn to walk according to the standard of Jesus in the ministry of healing.

Jesus said in John 14:12 that whoever believes in Him would do the same works and even greater works. Through The Healing Academy, it is our goal to raise the standard of the healing ministry in the Church up to the standard of Jesus Himself and manifest the ministry of Jesus in the marketplace.

The Healing Academy is available by video training series as well as in person training. For more information, please visit:

www.ChadGonzales.com

Other Books By The Author

Aliens
An Alternate Reality
Eight Percent
Fearless
God's Will Is You Healed
Making Right Decisions
Naturally Supernatural
Possessors Of Life
The Freedom Of Forgiveness
Think Like Jesus
What's Next
Walking In The Miraculous: a 30 day devotional